B♭ Edition

for TRUMPET, TENOR/SOPRAN...

10 ~e~a~s~y~ JAZZ DUETS

by JOHN LA PORTA with GREG NIELSEN,
Coordinator/Editor

TABLE OF CONTENTS

ISBN-10: 0-7692-3025-3
ISBN-13: 978-0-7692-3025-2

Introduction

The compact disc and book included in this package are designed to provide instrumentalists of all ages an opportunity to play duets in a variety of jazz styles. **10 EASY JAZZ DUETS** is published for the following instruments:

C Edition	Flute, Guitar, Violin, Vibraharp, Piano
B♭ Edition	Trumpet, Tenor/Soprano Sax, Clarinet
E♭ Edition	Alto Sax, Baritone Sax
Bass Clef Edition	Trombone, Acoustic/Electric Bass

A compact disc is included, making it possible for any individual to play the duets alone. Sections for improvising with a rhythm section are also provided. Chord symbols are provided for those who wish to improvise, and the CD includes a section for that purpose. The chord progressions have been patterned after the Blues and standard songs like HONEYSUCKLE ROSE, DOXY, FLY ME TO THE MOON, 'S WONDERFUL, SOMEDAY MY PRINCE WILL COME, and STRIKE UP THE BAND. One of the duets is based on inspiration from a Duke Ellington composition entitled DELTA SERENADE. The format after each tune suggests a form to use with the CD.

For performance or practice, a live jazz rhythm section (Piano, Bass, Drums, Guitar) can also be used with the book. These players should read the chord symbols in the C and Bass Clef editions.

These books are written in compatible keys so that any duet combination is possible. For example, an Alto Sax player and a Trombone player can play a duet together if the Alto plays the top line in the E♭ book and the Trombone plays the same piece using the bottom line in the Bass Clef book.

The music in this text offers a variety of uses and combinations. It is helpful to use the duets as a graduated study method with teacher supervision.

SOLO PRACTICE PROCEDURES WITH CD

1. Listen carefully to the compact disc. Play the CD of the tune you want to learn several times. Sing unison along with the CD when you can.

2. Before you play along with the CD, sight-read at a tempo that will allow you to play through the entire tune without stopping.

3. Work out trouble spots, pay attention to dynamics, accents, articulation marks and ghost notes, etc. Use the play along performance as your guide.

4. Play along with the CD when you feel you can play through the duet without stopping. First play unison with the CD, and listen to it as you play. Then, follow the written directions and play the B Section with the CD.

5. To improvise, play through the entire arrangement. The 3rd, 4th, and 5th choruses are specifically arranged for that purpose.

DUET PRACTICE PROCEDURES WITH CD

The book and CD can also be used by two individuals to play together. Individuals playing similar instruments can play these duets together using only one book. Two instruments which sound different pitches when reading the same note can also play the duets by using books corresponding to their instrument. (i.e. Flute must use the C Treble book while a B♭ Clarinet, B♭ Trumpet or B♭ Tenor Saxophone must use a B♭ book). These duets can also be played by unlike instruments who sound the same pitch when reading (Piano and Vibes, Violin and Flute, Flute and Guitar, etc.) The fact that a Guitar sounds an octave lower than written has been considered and should not be a problem.

1. Both players should play through the entire A Section at a comfortable tempo without the CD until it can be performed with accuracy. Do the same with the B Section (unison playing helps define rhythmic and melodic shape, and gives insight to the musical content in both sections).

2. Divide the sections - one player playing A Section while the other plays B Section. Reverse sections.

3. If both players want to play with the CD, turn the balance button to remove the melody then play both sections with the rhythm section. If improvising, play the duet on the first chorus, then take turns playing the four improvising choruses. Follow the directions for completing the arrangement after the last improvised chorus.

SOLO DUET PRACTICE PROCEDURES WITH LIVE RHYTHM

Any melody instrument can play the A Section of any of the jazz duets with a live rhythm section (Piano/Guitar, Bass and Drums) as long as the proper books are used. If necessary, copy the chord symbols (from the C books) for the Bass and Guitar and allow the Drummer to see your section to keep track of the form of the duet being played.

Any two instruments can play the A and B Sections with live rhythm sections by following the instructions provided for improvising with each jazz duet. If unlike instruments are involved, it may be necessary to acquire a set of C, Bass Clef, B♭ and E♭ books.

Follow the instructions provided for improvising that accompany each jazz duet. If you wish to play longer solos, direct the rhythm section to play additional choruses in the C Section provided for improvising. When two or more soloists are involved, pre-determine the playing order of the soloists.

REHEARSAL PROCEDURES FOR JAZZ WORKSHOP

Any combination of melody instruments can be used.

1. All instruments sight read through the A Section then through the B Section in unison.

2. Work on phrasing - still in unison.

3. Divide the instruments equally into two sections, one playing the A Section while the other group plays the B Section.

4. Work on trouble spots then perform the entire tune.

5. Work on the thematic material in much the same manner as directed above.

6. Work on rhythm section problems such as developing a group time sense, bass lines, piano/guitar comping etc. (Note: If you have a Piano, and Guitar, avoid comping problems by not having them play backgrounds for soloists at the same time).

7. Follow the procedures suggested for extended improvising that accompany each jazz duet.

4

The C. T. Calypso

JOHN LaPORTA

FORMAT - MUSIC + YOU

1. Play top line first chorus.
2. Play bottom line second chorus.
3. Improvise for three choruses at letter "C"
4. D.C. al Fine - play 1st and 2nd endings.

Wallerin' Around

JOHN LaPORTA

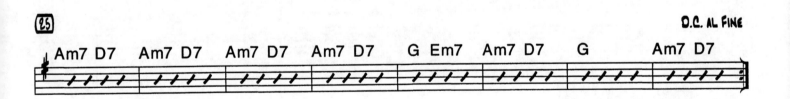

FORMAT - MUSIC + YOU

1. Play top line first chorus.
2. Play bottom line second chorus.
3. Improvise for the next three choruses at letter "C".
4. On D.C., Play top line to Fine. Observe repeat.

What Moxie!

JOHN LaPORTA

NOTE: AFTER SOLO CHORUSES, PLAY LETTER "X" TO FINE.

FORMAT - MUSIC + YOU

1. Play top line first chorus.
2. Play bottom line second chorus.
3. Improvise for three choruses at letter "C".
4. After last solo chorus, start at letter "X" and play until Fine.

To the Moon

JOHN LaPORTA

FORMAT - MUSIC + YOU

1. Play top line first chorus.
2. Play bottom line second chorus.
3. Improvise for three choruses at letter "C".
4. After last solo chorus, D.C. al Fine. Observe Repeat

Blues in "C"

JOHN LaPORTA

NOTE: AFTER 4TH SOLO CHORUS, GO TO "X" SHOUT CHORUS.

NOTE: D.C. (DA CAPO) GO BACK TO THE BEGINNING AND PLAY TOP LINE TO FINE (END).

FORMAT - MUSIC + YOU

1. Play top line on first chorus.
2. Play bottom line on second chorus.
3. Improvise for four choruses at "C".
4. Play "Shout Chorus" after solo.
5. D.C. Play top line to Fine.

Wonders!

JOHN LaPORTA

FORMAT - MUSIC + YOU

1. Play top line first chorus.
2. Play bottom line second chorus.
3. Improvise for the next three choruses at letter "C".
4. After last solo, D.C. to Fine. Play top line.

If You Don't Succeed!

JOHN LaPORTA

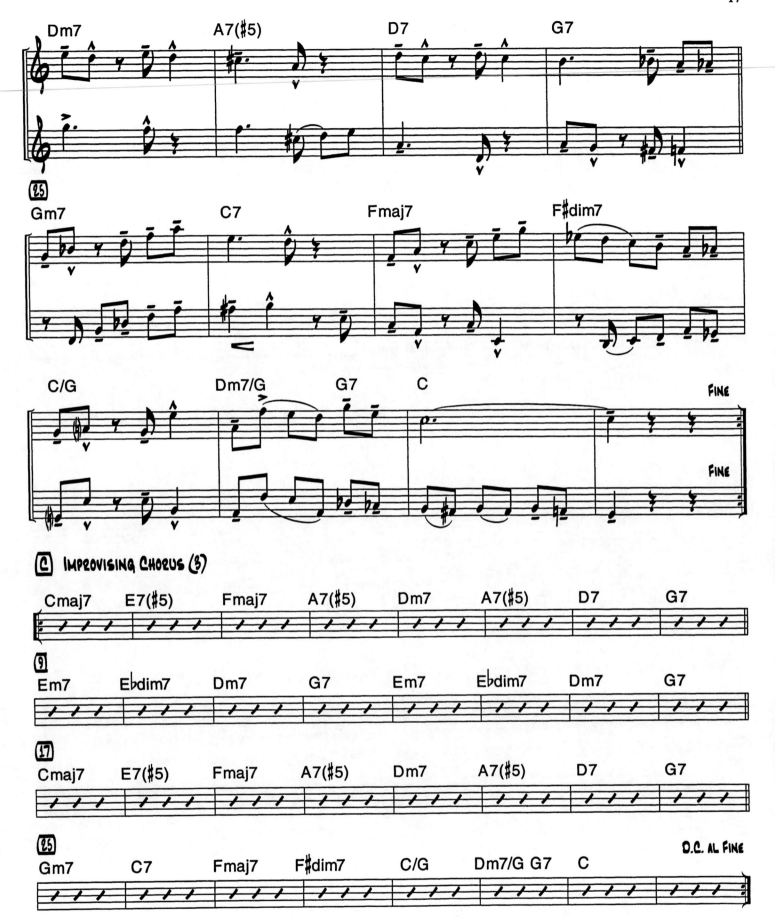

FORMAT - MUSIC + YOU

1. Play top line first chorus.
2. Play bottom line second chorus.
3. Improvise for the next three choruses.
4. After last solo chorus, play top line to Fine.
   Ritard the last two measures.

Will You Be Good to Me?

JOHN LaPORTA

19

FORMAT - MUSIC + YOU

1. Play top line on first chorus.
2. Play bottom line on second chorus.
3. Improvise for three choruses at letter "C".
4. After last chorus, D.C. al Fine. Observe Repeat.

Minor Ambiguity

JOHN LaPORTA

FORMAT - MUSIC + YOU

1. Play top line on first chorus.
2. Play bottom line on second chorus.
3. Improvise for three choruses at "C".
4. D.C., Play top line to Fine. (Observe repeat)

Cat Fight

JOHN LaPORTA

FORMAT - MUSIC + YOU

1. Play top line first chorus.
2. Play bottom line second chorus.
3. Improvise for the next three choruses.
4. After last solo, D.C. to Fine. Play top line.